Harvey Milk

By United Library

https://campsite.bio/unitedlibrary

Table of Contents

Disclaimer

This biography book is a work of nonfiction based on the public life of a famous person. The author has used publicly available information to create this work. While the author has thoroughly researched the subject and attempted to depict it accurately, it is not meant to be an exhaustive study of the subject. The views expressed in this book are those of the author alone and do not necessarily reflect those of any organization associated with the subject. This book should not be taken as an endorsement, legal advice, or any other form of professional advice. This book was written for entertainment purposes only.

Introduction

Explore the captivating life of Harvey Bernard Milk, an American political pioneer born on May 22, 1930, who defied social norms by becoming the first openly gay man to be elected to public office in California. Originally from New York, Milk dealt with his homosexuality during his formative years, navigating a path marked by secrecy and discretion. The transformative influence of the 1960s counterculture led him to re-evaluate his conservative beliefs, paving the way for a remarkable journey.

In 1972, Milk made San Francisco his home, opening a camera store in the heart of the growing LGBTQ+ haven in the Castro district. Undeterred by resistance from established gay political circles, he launched a vigorous campaign for city supervisor in 1973, earning the nickname "Mayor of Castro Street". Despite initial setbacks, Milk's perseverance and charisma catapulted him to political prominence.

Elected city supervisor in 1977, Milk became a staunch defender of LGBTQ+ rights, spearheading groundbreaking anti-discrimination legislation. Tragically, his life was cut short on November 27, 1978, when he and Mayor George Moscone were assassinated. Milk's legacy persists as an enduring symbol of courage, activism and the ongoing struggle for equality. This biography explores the multifaceted journey of a visionary leader, celebrating Milk's indomitable spirit and his pivotal role in LGBTQ+ history.

Harvey Milk

Harvey Bernard Milk (Woodmere, May 22, 1930 - San Francisco, November 27, 1978) was an American politician and gay activist. He was the first openly gay man to be elected to public office in California, as a San Francisco city supervisor. Politics and gay activism were not Milk's first interests; he didn't feel the need to be open about his homosexuality or participate in civil causes until he was around 40, after his experiences with the 1960s counterculture.Milk moved from New York to take up residence in San Francisco in 1972, amid a migration of gay men moving to the Castro in the 1970s. He took advantage of the neighborhood's growing political and economic power to promote his interests, and ran unsuccessfully for political office three times. His theatrical campaigns gave him growing popularity, and Milk obtained a seat as a city supervisor in 1977 as a result of the broader social changes the city was facing.

Milk served for 11 months and was responsible for passing a strict gay rights law for the city. On November 27, 1978, Milk and Mayor George Moscone were assassinated by Dan White, another city supervisor, who had recently resigned but wanted his job back. Conflicts between the liberal tendencies that were responsible for Milk's election and the conservative resistance to these changes were evident in the events following the assassinations.

Despite his short career in politics, Milk became an icon in San Francisco and "a martyr for gay rights", according to University of San Francisco professor Peter Novak. In 2002, Milk was called "the most famous and most significant openly LGBT politician ever elected in the United States". Anne Kronenberg, his last campaign manager, wrote of him: "What set Harvey apart from you or me was that he was a visionary. He envisioned a virtuous world inside his head, and then he took action to create it for real, for all of us."

There are several works that pay tribute to Milk, including a 1984 Oscar-winning documentary. In 2008, the film *Milk* was released, telling the story of Harvey from his arrival in San Francisco to his death. Directed by Gus Van Sant, with Sean Penn in the role of Milk, it received eight Oscar nominations, of which it won Best Actor and Best Original Screenplay.

Early years

Childhood

Harvey Bernard Milk was born in Woodmere, Long Island, on May 22, 1930, to William and Minerva Karns Milk. He was the youngest child of Lithuanian Jewish parents and the grandson of a salesman, Morris Milk, who owned a grocery store and helped organize the first synagogue in the area. As a child, Milk was teased for his protruding ears, large nose and disproportionate feet, and tended to attract attention as a class clown. He played soccer at school, and developed a passion for opera; in his teens, he discovered his homosexuality, but kept it a secret. His name in the high school yearbook reads "Glimpy Milk - and they say that WOMEN are never at a loss for words".

Milk graduated from Bay Shore High School in Bay Shore in 1947 and attended New York State College for Teachers in Albany (now the State University of New York at Albany) from 1947 to 1951, majoring in mathematics. He wrote for the college newspaper and gained a reputation as a sociable and friendly student. None of his friends at school or college suspected that he was gay. As one colleague recalled, "He was never seen as a possible queer - that's what you called him then - he was a man who liked men's things (*a man's man*)".

Early career

After graduation, Milk joined the US Navy during the Korean War. He served aboard the submarine rescue ship USS *Kittiwake* as a diving officer. He was later transferred to the San Diego Naval Base to serve as a diving instructor. In 1955, he was discharged from the Navy at the rank of lieutenant.

Milk's early career was marked by frequent changes; years later, he would have delighted in talking about his metamorphosis from a middle-class Jewish boy. He began teaching at George W. Hewlett High School on Long Island. In 1956, he met Joe Campbell on the beach at Jacob Riis Park, a popular spot for gay men in Queens. Campbell was seven years younger than Milk, and Milk fell hard for him. Even after they moved in together, Milk would write Campbell romantic notes and poems. With boredom growing rapidly, they decided to move to Dallas, Texas, but were unhappy there and returned to New York, where Milk got a job as an actuarial statistician in an insurance company". Campbell and Milk separated after almost six years; this would be their longest relationship.

Milk tried to separate his early romantic life from his family and work. Once again bored and single in New York, he considered moving to Miami to marry a lesbian friend "so that they would appear to be a couple and each wouldn't be a problem in the other's way". However, he remained in New York and lived gay relationships in secret. In 1962, Milk became involved with Craig Rodwell, who was ten years younger. Although Milk courted Rodwell ardently, waking him up every morning with a phone call and sending him messages, Milk was discouraged by Rodwell's participation in the Mattachine Society of New York, a gay activist organization. When Rodwell was arrested walking in Riis Park, accused of inciting a riot and wearing indecent attire (the law required men's bathing suits to extend from above the navel to below the thighs), he spent three days in jail. The relationship soon ended when Milk became aware of Rodwell's tendency to provoke the police.

Milk abruptly left his job as an insurance salesman to become an investigator at Bache & Company, a Wall Street firm. He was promoted several times, despite his tendency to offend senior members of the company by ignoring their advice and showing off his own success. Although he was skilled at his job, colleagues detected that Milk's heart wasn't in his work. He began a relationship with Jack Galen McKinley and recruited him to fight against the increased presence of the state in the economy, persuading McKinley to work on the presidential campaign of conservative Republican Barry Goldwater. Their relationship was turbulent: McKinley was prone to depression and often threatened to commit suicide if Milk didn't pay enough attention to him. To help McKinley, Milk took him to the hospital where Joe Campbell, Milk's ex-boyfriend, was recovering from a suicide attempt after his lover - a man named Billy Sipple - left him. Milk had remained friends with Campbell, who had incorporated the Greenwich Village *avant-garde* scene, and couldn't understand why Campbell's despondency was cause enough to consider suicide as an option.

Route to Castro Street

San Francisco's Eureka Valley, where Market and Castro streets intersect, was for decades an Irish Catholic neighborhood of manual laborers linked to San Francisco's Most Holy Redeemer Parish. In the early 1960s, however, new families left the neighborhood and moved to the San Francisco Bay Area, and the city's economic base was greatly affected when factories moved to cheaper nearby locations. Mayor Joseph Alioto, proud of his background and his working-class supporters, based his political career on welcoming entrepreneurs and attracting a Roman Catholic cardinal to the city. Many manual laborers - often Alioto supporters - lost their jobs when large corporations focused on the service industry replaced jobs in factories and on the dry dock. San

Francisco was "a city of villages": a decentralized city with ethnic enclaves, each surrounding its own main street.

While the central area developed, the neighborhoods suffered, including Castro Street. The stores of the Most Holy Redeemer Parish closed, and houses were abandoned and sealed off. In 1963, real estate prices collapsed when most working-class families tried to sell their homes quickly after a gay bar opened in the neighborhood. Hippies, attracted by the free-love ideals of the Haight-Ashbury area but repulsed by its crime rate, bought some of the cheap Victorian-style houses.

Since the end of the Second World War, the main port city, San Francisco, had been home to a considerable number of gay men expelled from the armed forces who had given up on returning home and facing ostracism. By 1969, San Francisco had more gays per capita than any other American city; when the National Institute of Mental Health asked the Kinsey Institute to examine homosexuals, the institute chose San Francisco as its focus. Milk and McKinley were among the thousands of gay men attracted to San Francisco. McKinley was a stagehand for Tom O' Horgan, a director who began his career in experimental theater, but soon reached the much larger Broadway productions. They arrived in 1969 with the traveling Broadway company that toured with the musical *Hair*. McKinley received an offer to work on the New York production of *Jesus Christ Superstar*, and their stormy relationship came to an end. The city attracted Milk so much that he decided to stay there, working for an investment company. In 1970, increasingly frustrated by the political climate following the US invasion of Cambodia, Milk let his hair grow. When ordered to cut it, he refused and was fired.

Milk wandered from California to Texas to New York without a steady job or a plan. In New York he became involved with O'Horgan's theater company as a "general helper", signing on as associate producer for *Lenny* and Eve Merriam's *Inner City.* The period spent living with people who shared San Francisco's hippie atmosphere had greatly reduced Milk's conservatism. A *New York Times* story about O'Horgan described Milk as the "sad-looking man - another aging hippie with long, long hair, wearing faded denim pants and pretty beads." Craig Rodwell read the description of the once uptight man and wondered if it could be the same person. One of Milk's Wall Street friends worried that he seemed to have no plan or future, but remembered Milk's attitude: "I think he was happier than at any other time in his life that I've seen."

Milk met Scott Smith, 18 years younger, and began another relationship. He and Smith, now indistinguishable from other long-haired, bearded hippies, returned to San

Francisco and lived on the money they had saved. In 1972, a roll of film that Milk had left to be developed broke; with his last thousand dollars, he opened a photo store on Castro Street.

Changing policies

At the end of the 1960s, the Society for Individual Rights (SIR) and Daughters of Bilitis (DOB) began to fight against police harassment of gay bars and inducement to commit crimes in San Francisco. Oral sex was still a serious offense, and in 1970, almost 90 people in the city were arrested for it. Subject to eviction if caught having homosexual relations in a rented apartment, and reluctant to face arrest in gay bars, some men started having sex in public parks at night. Mayor Alioto asked the police to focus their attention on the parks, hoping that the decision would please the archdiocese and its Catholic supporters. In 1971, 2,800 gay men were arrested for public sex in San Francisco. For comparison, New York recorded only 63 arrests for the same offense that year. All arrests on moral charges required registration as sexual assault.

Congressman Phillip Burton, Assemblymember Willie Brown, and other California politicians recognized the growing influence and organization of homosexuals in the city, and courted their votes by attending meetings of gay and lesbian organizations. Brown proposed legalizing consensual sex between adults in 1969 but was unsuccessful. SIR was also sought out by popular moderate Supervisor Dianne Feinstein in her bid to be elected mayor, in opposition to Alioto. Former police officer Richard Hongisto worked for ten years to change the conservative outlook of the San Francisco Police Department, while also actively appealing to the gay community, which responded by raising significant funds for his campaign for sheriff. Although Feinstein was unsuccessful, Hongisto's victory in 1971 showed the political weight of the gay community.

SIR had become powerful enough for political maneuvering. In 1971, CRS members Jim Foster, Rick Stokes and *Advocate* editor David Goodstein created the Alice B. Toklas Memorial Democratic Club. Toklas, known simply as "*Alice*". The *Alice* approached liberal politicians to persuade them to sponsor bills, which proved to be a successful strategy when in 1972 Del Martin and Phyllis Lyon obtained Feinstein's support for an ordinance banning employment discrimination on the basis of sexual orientation. *Alice* chose Stokes to run for a relatively unimportant seat on the community's education committee. Although Stokes received 45,000 votes, he was quiet, unassuming, and didn't win. Foster, however, rose to national prominence by being the first openly gay man to speak at a political convention. His speech at the 1972 Democratic National Convention ensured that his voice, according to San Francisco politicians, was the one to be heard when they wanted the opinions, and especially the votes, of the gay community.

One day in 1973 a state employee walked into Milk's store, Castro Camera, informing him that he owed 100 dollars in sales tax. Milk was incredulous and yelled at the man about the rights of business owners; after he complained for weeks at state offices, the amount was reduced to 30 dollars. Milk was showing his dissatisfaction with the government's priorities when a teacher came into his store to ask for a projector because the equipment in the schools wasn't working. Friends also recall that at the same time they had to stop him from kicking the television when US Attorney General John N. Mitchell gave the consistent "I don't recall" answers during the Watergate hearings in the US Senate. Milk decided the time had come to run for city supervisor. He later said, "I finally got to the point where I knew I had to get involved or shut up."

Campaigns

Milk's reception by gay political leaders in San Francisco was frosty. Jim Foster, who until then had been active in gay politics for ten years, took offense at the newcomer's request to support him for a position as prestigious as city supervisor. Foster told Milk, "There's an old saying in the Democratic party: *You can't dance unless you put the chairs in.* I've never seen you put the chairs in. Milk was furious at the patronizing censorship, and the dialogue marked the beginning of an antagonistic relationship between *Alice* and Harvey Milk. Some gay bar owners, still struggling against police harassment and unhappy with what they saw as *Alice*'s timid approach to the city's established authorities, decided to support him.

Although he had wandered throughout his life up to that point, Milk had now found his vocation, according to journalist Frances FitzGerald, who called him an "innate politician". At first, his inexperience was clear. He tried politics without money, support and staff, and relied instead on his message of sound financial management, promoting individuals over big corporations and government. He supported the reorganization of supervisor elections so that the citywide electoral college would be reduced to a district-wide scope, which would reduce the influence of money and give neighborhoods more control over their representatives in city government. He also followed a social liberal platform, opposing government interference in private sexual matters and supporting the legalization of marijuana. His fiery, over-the-top speeches and well-known media skills won him significant crowds during the 1973 election. He won 16,900 votes - winning spectacularly in the Castro district and other liberal neighborhoods - finishing tenth out of 32 candidates. If the elections had been reorganized to allow districts to elect their own supervisors, he would have won.

Mayor of Castro Street

Milk showed an affinity for building alliances early on in his political career. The Teamsters union wanted to promote a strike against beer distributors - Coors in particular - who refused to sign a collective bargaining agreement. An organizer asked Milk to help out in gay bars; in return, Milk asked the organization to employ more gay drivers. A few days later, Milk called gay bars in and around the Castro district, urging them to refuse to sell the beer. With the support of Arab and Chinese grocery stores, which the Teamsters had also recruited, the boycott was hugely successful. Milk found a strong political ally in the unions, and it was around this time that he began calling himself "The Mayor of Castro Street". As Castro Street grew, Milk's reputation followed suit. Tom O' Horgan observed, "Harvey spent most of his life looking for a stage. On Castro Street he finally found it".

Tensions between the senior citizens of Most Holy Redeemer parish and gay immigration entering the Castro district escalated in 1973. When two gay men tried to open an antique store, the Eureka Valley Merchants Association (EVMA) tried to prevent them from receiving a business license. Milk and some other gay businessmen founded the Castro Village Association, with Milk as president. He often repeated his philosophy that homosexuals should buy from gay merchants. He organized the Castro Street Fair in 1974 to attract more customers to the area. More than 5,000 people attended, and some of the EVMA members were shocked; they did more business at the Castro Street Fair than on any day up to that point.

Serious candidate

Although he was a newcomer to the Castro district, Milk had shown leadership in the small community. He was beginning to be taken seriously as a candidate and decided to run again for supervisor in 1975. He reconsidered his approach and cut his long hair, promised to stop smoking marijuana and vowed never to go to a gay sauna again. His campaign won the support of truck drivers, firefighters and unions. Castro Camera became the center of activity in the neighborhood. Milk often pulled people off the street to work with him on his campaigns - many later discovered that this was only because they were the kind of men Milk found attractive.

Milk facilitated the support of small businesses and the growth of neighborhoods. Since 1968, Mayor Alioto had attracted large corporations to the city, which critics labeled the "Manhattanization of San Francisco". When jobs for less qualified people were replaced by the service industry, Alioto's weakened political base allowed the rise of new leaders to the city's political offices. George Moscone was elected mayor. Moscone had previously collaborated to repeal the sodomy law that year in the California legislature. He acknowledged Milk's influence on his election by visiting Milk's campaign night central committee, thanking him personally, and offering him a position as a city commissioner. Milk won seventh place in the election, just one position short of the one needed to be elected supervisor. Liberal politicians won the positions of mayor, district attorney and sheriff.

Despite the new leadership in the city, there were still conservative strongholds. One of Moscone's first acts was to appoint a police chief to put the San Francisco Police Department (SFPD) in order. He chose Charles Gain, against the wishes of the SFPD. Most members disliked Gain for criticizing the police in the press for racial insensitivity and alcohol abuse on the job, instead of working within the command structure to change attitudes. At the mayor's request, Gain made it clear that gay officers would be welcome in the department; this became national news. Police officers subordinate to Gain expressed their hatred of him and the mayor for betraying them.

Campaigning for the California Assembly

Keeping his promise to Milk, newly elected mayor George Moscone appointed him to the License Appeals Committee in 1976, making him the first openly gay city commissioner in the United States. Milk, meanwhile, considered running for a seat in the California Legislature. The district was heavily tilted in his favor, being based in the neighborhoods surrounding Castro Street, where Milk's supporters voted. In the previous election for supervisor, Milk had received more votes than the current representative in the assembly. However, Moscone had made a deal with the *speaker of* the assembly that another candidate should run for the post - Art Agnos. In addition, by order of the mayor, no appointed or elected office holder could run while in office.

Milk spent five weeks on the License Appeals Committee until Moscone was forced to remove him when he announced he was running for the California Legislature. Rick Stokes replaced him. Milk's ouster and the secret deal made between Moscone, the Speaker of the Legislative Assembly and Agnos fueled his campaign as he assumed the posture of political victim. He shouted that the highest authorities in the city and state government were against him. He complained that the gay political summit, particularly the Alice Club, didn't support him; he referred to Jim Foster and Stokes as Uncle Tom gays (subservient gays). He enthusiastically adopted the headline of a local independent weekly magazine: "Harvey Milk against The Machine".

Milk's role as a representative of San Francisco's gay community expanded during this period. On September 22, 1975, President Gerald Ford was visiting San Francisco, walking from his hotel to his car. In the crowd, Sara Jane Moore raised a gun to shoot him. A former US Marine walking next to her grabbed her arm, causing the gun to shoot into the ground. The man was Oliver "Bill" Sipple, who years earlier had abandoned Milk's ex-boyfriend, Joe Campbell, which had motivated her suicide attempt. Sipple, who had left the military due to psychiatric disability, lived in the Tenderloin neighborhood, and immediately gained national prominence. Sipple refused to call himself a hero and wouldn't reveal his sexual orientation. Milk, however, took the opportunity to reinforce his thesis that public perception of gays would be improved if they came out of the closet. He told a friend: "This is too good an opportunity. For the first time we can show that gays do heroic things, not just all these scandals about child molestation and public displays in toilets." Milk contacted a newspaper.

Several days later Herb Caen, a columnist for *The San Francisco Chronicle*, exposed Sipple as gay and a friend of Milk. The news was reported in newspapers nationwide, and Milk's name was included in many of the stories. *Time* magazine called Milk a leader of the gay community in San Francisco. Sipple, meanwhile, was harassed by reporters, as was his family. His mother, a faithful Baptist in Detroit, refused to speak to him. Although he had been involved in the gay community for years, even participating in gay parades, Sipple sued the *Chronicle* for invasion of privacy. President Ford sent Sipple a thank-you note for saving his life. Milk said that Sipple's sexual orientation was the reason he had only received a note, not an invitation to the White House.

The continuation of Milk's campaign, conducted from the Castro Camera window, was a study in disorganization. Although the volunteers were happy and productive sending out mass mailings, Milk's notes and lists of volunteers were kept on scraps of paper. When the campaign needed funds, the money came from the cash register without any concern for bookkeeping. An 11-year-old girl from the neighborhood led gay men and Irish grandmothers in the campaign's work, despite her mother's discouragement. Milk himself was hyperactive and prone to irrational temper tantrums, only to recover quickly and shout excitedly about something else. Many of his extravagant speeches were directed at his lover, Scott Smith, who was becoming disillusioned with the man who no longer resembled the calm hippie he had fallen in love with.

If the candidate was a maniac, he was also dedicated and full of good humor, as well as having a particular talent for attracting media attention. He spent a lot of time enlisting voters and shaking hands at bus stops and in movie lines. He took every opportunity to promote himself. He enjoyed running the campaign immensely, and its success was evident. With a large number of volunteers, he had dozens at the rest stops along the crowded Market Street walkway serving as human bulletin boards holding up "Milk for Assembly" signs as public transport users headed into the heart of the city to work. He distributed his campaign material wherever he could, including one of the most influential political groups in the city: Peoples Temple. Milk's volunteers took thousands of leaflets there, but returned with feelings of apprehension. Because the leader of Peoples Temple, Jim Jones, was politically powerful in San Francisco (and supported both candidates), Milk allowed temple members to handle his phones, and later spoke at the temple and defended Jones. But to his volunteers, he said: "Make sure you're always nice to Peoples Temple. If they ask you to do something, do it, and then send them a thank you note for asking you to do it. They are strange and dangerous, and you never want to be on their bad side."

The race was tight, and Milk lost by less than 4,000 votes. Agnos, however, taught Milk a valuable lesson when she criticized his campaign speeches as "a misfortune... You talk about how you're going to get rid of the bums, but how are you going to fix things - apart from hitting me? You shouldn't make your public depressed". As a consequence of his defeat, Milk, realizing that Toklas' club would never support him politically, helped found the San Francisco Gay Democratic Club.

Historically broader forces

The fledgling gay rights movement still had to encounter organized opposition in the United States. In 1977, some well-connected gay activists in Miami were able to pass a civil law ordinance that made discrimination based on sexual orientation illegal in Dade County. A well-organized group of conservative fundamentalist Christians reacted, led by singer Anita Bryant. Their campaign was titled Save Our Children, and Bryant argued that the ordinance infringed on her right to teach biblical morality to children. Bryant and the campaign collected 64,000 signatures to put the issue to a countywide vote. With funds raised in part by the Florida Citrus Commission, of which Bryant was the spokesperson, they ran television advertisements contrasting the Orange Bowl Parade with San Francisco's Gay Liberation Day Parade, indicating that Dade County would be transformed into a "hotbed of homosexuality" where "men ... jump around with little boys".

Jim Foster, then the most powerful political organizer in San Francisco, went to Miami to help gay activists as election day approached, and a nationwide orange juice boycott was organized. The Save Our Children campaign's message was influential, and the result was a crushing defeat for the gay activists; in the largest turnout for a special election in Dade County history, 70% voted to repeal the law.

Just politics

Christian conservatives were inspired by their victory, and saw an opportunity for a new and effective political cause. Gay activists were shocked to see how little support they had received. A spontaneous demonstration of more than 3,000 Castro residents formed the night of the vote on the Dade County law. The gays and lesbians were simultaneously angry, chanting "Out of the bars and into the streets!", and jubilant in their passionate and powerful response. *The San Francisco Examiner* reported that members of the crowd were pulling others out of bars along Castro and Polk streets to join the demonstration. Milk led the demonstrators that night on a five-mile (8 km) route through the city, constantly moving, aware that if they stopped for too long there would be a riot. He declared, "This is the power of the gay community. Anita is going to create a national gay force". The activists, however, had little time to recover, because the scene was repeated when civil rights laws were overturned by voters in Saint Paul (Minnesota), Wichita

(Kansas) and Eugene (Oregon) throughout 1977 and into 1978.

California state senator John Briggs saw an opportunity in the campaign of fundamentalist Christians. He planned to run for governor of California in 1978, and was impressed by the turnout he saw in Miami. When Briggs returned to Sacramento, he drafted a bill that would ban gays and lesbians from teaching in public schools throughout California. Briggs claimed privately that he had nothing against gays, telling Randy Shilts, "That's politics. Just politics." Random attacks on gays increased in the Castro. When the police response was deemed inadequate, gay groups patrolled the neighborhood themselves, on the alert against attackers. On June 21, 1977, a gay man named Robert Hillsborough died from 15 stab wounds when his attackers surrounded him and shouted in chorus "Faggot!" Both Mayor Moscone and Hillsborough's mother blamed Anita Bryant and John Briggs. A week before the incident, Briggs had defended his views at a press conference at San Francisco City Hall, where he called the city a "sexual trash heap" because of homosexuals. Weeks later, 250,000 people attended San Francisco's Gay Freedom Day Parade, the largest number ever seen at a gay pride event to that date.

In November 1976, San Francisco voters had decided to reorganize the supervisor elections to choose them in each district instead of keeping the vote open to the entire city. Harvey Milk quickly qualified as the leading candidate in District 5, around Castro Street.

Last campaign

Anita Bryant's public campaign against homosexuality and the multiple challenges to gay rights laws across the country fueled gay politicians in San Francisco. Seventeen candidates in the Castro district registered for the next election for supervisor; more than half of them were gay. *The New York Times* revealed a legitimate gay invasion in San Francisco, estimating that the gay population was 100,000 to 200,000 out of a total of 750,000 people. The Castro Village Association had grown to 90 business owners; the local bank branch, previously the smallest branch in the city, had become the largest, forcing the construction of a wing to accommodate its new clients. Randy Shilts, Milk's biographer, noted that these broader forces of history fueled his campaign.

Milk's strongest competitor was the quiet, thoughtful lawyer Rick Stokes, who was backed by the Alice B. Toklas Memorial Democratic Club. Toklas. Stokes had revealed about his homosexuality much earlier than Milk, and had experienced harsher treatment, once being hospitalized and forced to endure electroshock therapy. Milk, however, was more outspoken about the role of gays and their issues in San Francisco politics. Stokes was quoted as saying "I'm just a businessman who happens to be gay" and expressed the view that every normal person could equally be homosexual. Milk's contrasting populist philosophy was repeated to *The New York Times*: "We don't want nice liberals, we want gays representing gays... I represent the gay population of the streets - the 14-year-old gay runaway from San Antonio. We have to make up for hundreds of years of persecution. We have to give hope to this poor runaway child from San Antonio. They go to the bars because the churches are hostile. They need hope! They need a piece of the pie!".

Other causes were equally important to Milk: he focused on bigger and cheaper nurseries, free public transport and the creation of a committee of civilians to keep an eye on the police. He advanced important neighborhood issues at every opportunity. He used the same maniacal tactics as in previous election campaigns: human bulletin boards, hours of handshaking and dozens of speeches inviting gay people to hope. This time, even *The San Francisco Chronicle* endorsed him for supervisor. He won with 30% of the vote against sixteen other candidates, and after his victory became clear, he arrived on Castro Street on the back of his campaign manager's motorcycle - escorted by Sheriff Richard Hongisto - to what one newspaper article described as a "tumultuous and moving welcome".

Milk had recently taken a new lover, a young man called Jack Lira, who was often drunk in public, and was often just removed from political events by Milk's aides. Since the election campaign for the California Assembly, Milk had been receiving increasingly violent death threats. Aware that his visibility marked him out as a target for assassination, he recorded on a tape what he wished would happen if he were assassinated, adding: "If a bullet enters my brain, let the bullet destroy every closet door".

Supervisor

Milk's pledge made national headlines as he became the first openly gay man in the United States not to have previously held office to win election to public office. He compared himself to pioneering African-American baseball player Jackie Robinson and walked to City Hall arm in arm with Jack Lira, declaring "You can stand around and throw bricks at City Hall asshole or you can take it over. Well, we're here". Castro's district wasn't the only one to promote someone new to city politics. The single mother (Carol Ruty Silver), the Chinese-American (Gordon Lau), and the African-American (Ella Hill Hutch) were all first-timers to the city oath along with Milk, as was Daniel White, a former police officer and firefighter, who spoke of how proud he was that his grandmother could see him taking the oath.

Milk's energy, penchant for embellishment and unpredictability sometimes exasperated Dianne Feinstein, president of the Board of Supervisors. In her first meeting with Mayor Moscone, Milk called herself "queen number one" and imposed on Moscone that he would have to use Milk instead of the Alice Club as a go-between if he wanted the city's gay votes - a quarter of San Francisco's voting population. Milk, meanwhile, became Moscone's closest ally on the Board of Supervisors. The biggest targets of Milk's ire were big corporations and real estate agents. He was furious when a garage building was planned to take the place of homes near the downtown area, and an attempt was made to pass a tax so that office workers who lived outside the city and drove to work every day would have to pay for the city services they used. Milk was often willing to vote against Feinstein and other more staid Council members. He initially agreed with his fellow supervisor Dan White, whose district was two miles south of the Castro, that a mental health clinic for troubled teens should not be housed there in an old convent. However, after Milk learned more about the issue, he decided to change his vote, causing White to lose his case - one he had advocated for during his campaign. White didn't forget that. He opposed every initiative and issue supported by Milk.

Milk began his term by sponsoring a civil rights bill that banned discrimination based on sexual orientation. The law was called "the strictest and most comprehensive in the nation," and its passage demonstrated "the growing political power of homosexuals," according to *The New York Times*. Only Supervisor White voted against it; Mayor Moscone enthusiastically signed it into law with a light blue pen that Milk had given him for the occasion.

Milk's second bill focused on solving the number one problem, according to a recent survey in the city: dog excrement. Within the first month of taking office, he began working on a municipal law to require dog owners to pick up their animals' feces. Nicknamed the "pooper scooper law", its approval by the Board of Supervisors was widely covered by television and newspapers in San Francisco. Anne Kronenberg, Milk's campaign manager, called him "a master at figuring out what would get him news coverage". He invited the press to Duboce Park to explain why the law was necessary, and while the cameras were rolling, stepped on some undesirable material apparently by mistake. His aides, however, knew that he had gone to the park an hour before the press conference to look for the right place to walk in front of the cameras. The episode earned him the biggest fan mail of his tenure in politics and made national headlines.

Milk and Lira soon split up, but Lira called him a few weeks later and demanded that Milk come to her apartment. When Milk arrived, he saw that Lira had hanged himself. Already prone to severe depression, Lira had been upset by the campaigns of Anita Bryant and John Briggs.

The Briggs initiative

John Briggs was forced to drop out of the California gubernatorial race in 1978, but received enthusiastic support for Proposition 6, dubbed the Briggs Initiative. The proposed law would make it mandatory to fire gay teachers and any public school employee who supported gay rights. Briggs' messages supporting Proposition 6 were spread throughout California, and Harvey Milk attended every event Briggs organized. Milk also campaigned against the bill statewide and vowed that even if Briggs won in California, he wouldn't win in San Francisco. In their numerous debates, which until the end had been characterized by rapid challenges from both sides, Briggs maintained that homosexual teachers wanted to abuse children and recruit them. Milk responded with statistics compiled by law enforcement authorities presenting evidence that child sex abusers are mainly identified as heterosexuals, and rebuffed Briggs' arguments with jocular remarks: "If it were true that children imitate their teachers, you can be sure there would be a lot more nuns walking around."

Attendance at gay parades during the summer of 1978 in Los Angeles and San Francisco grew. A turnout of 250,000 to 375,000 people was estimated for San Francisco's Gay Freedom Day Parade; newspapers claimed that the larger numbers were due to John Briggs. Organizers asked participants to carry signs indicating their hometowns into the chambers to show how far people had come to live in the Castro district. Milk rode in an open car carrying a sign saying "I'm from Woodmere, NY". He gave a version of what became his most famous speech, the

"Hope Speech," which *The San Francisco Examiner* said "ignited the crowd."

Despite losses in gay rights battles across the country this year, he remained optimistic, saying that "Even if gays lose in these initiatives, people are still being educated. Because of Anita Bryant and Dade County, the whole country has been educated about homosexuality to a greater extent than ever before. The first step is always hostility, and after that you can sit down and talk about it."

Citing potential infringements on individual rights, former California Governor Ronald Reagan expressed his opposition to the proposal, as did Governor Jerry Brown and President Jimmy Carter, the latter in an explanation after a speech he gave in Sacramento. On November 7, 1978, the proposition lost by more than a million votes, surprising gay activists on election night. In San Francisco, seventy-five percent voted against it.

The murder

On November 10, 1978, ten months after being sworn in, White resigned his seat on the San Francisco Board of Supervisors, claiming that his annual salary of $9,600 was not enough to support his family. Milk had also felt the pinch of his diminishing income when he and Scott Smith were forced to close Castro Camera a month earlier. A few days later, White asked for his mandate back and Mayor Moscone initially agreed. However, further analysis - and the intervention of other supervisors - convinced the mayor to appoint someone more in line with the growing ethnic diversity of White's district and the liberal leanings of the Board of Supervisors. On November 18, news broke of the murder of California Congressman Leo Ryan, who was in Jonestown, Guyana, to check on the remote community built by Peoples Temple members who had moved from San Francisco. The next day, news arrived of the mass suicide of Peoples Temple members. The horror came gradually when the population of San Francisco learned that more than 400 residents of Jonestown were dead. Dan White commented to two advisors working for his reinstatement, "You see that? One day I'm on the cover and the next I'm immediately swept away". Soon the death toll in Guyana exceeded 900.

Moscone planned to announce White's replacement a few days later, on November 27, 1978. Half an hour before the press conference, Dan White entered City Hall through a basement window to avoid the metal detectors and went to Mayor Moscone's office. Witnesses heard shouting between White and Moscone, then gunshots. White shot the mayor once in the arm and then three times in the head after Moscone had fallen to the ground. White then walked quickly to his old office, reloading along the way his police-exclusive revolver with concave-tipped bullets, and intercepted Harvey Milk, asking him to come in for a moment. Dianne Feinstein heard shots and called the police. She found Milk face down on the floor, shot five times, including twice in the head at close range. Feinstein was shaking so badly that she needed support from the police chief after identifying both bodies. It was she who announced to the press, "Today San Francisco suffered a double tragedy of immense proportions. As president of the Board of Supervisors, it is my duty to inform you that both Mayor Moscone and Supervisor Harvey Milk have been shot and killed," then adding, after being drowned out by shouts of disbelief, "and the suspect is Supervisor Dan White." Milk was 48 years old and Moscone was 49.

Within an hour, White called his wife from a nearby diner, who found him in a church and accompanied him to the police, where White turned himself in. Many residents left flowers on the steps of the town hall. That evening, a spontaneous gathering began to form on Castro Street, moving towards City Hall in a candlelight vigil. The number of people was estimated at between 25,000 and 40,000, covering all of Market Street, stretching a mile and a half (2.4 km) from Castro Street. The next day, the bodies of Moscone and Milk were taken to the rotunda of City Hall where mourners paid their respects. Six thousand mourners attended the funeral ceremony for Mayor Moscone at St. Mary's Cathedral. Two ceremonies were held for Milk; a small one at Temple Emanu-El and a more boisterous one at the San Francisco theater.

"City in agony"

Shortly before, Mayor Moscone had increased security at City Hall because of the Jonestown suicides. Survivors in Guyana reported training sessions in preparation for the suicides, which Jones called "*White Nights*". Rumors about the murders of Moscone and Milk were thickened by the coincidence of Dan White's name and Jones' suicide preparations. A stunned district attorney called the murders so close to the Jonestown news "incomprehensible", but denied any connection. Governor Jerry Brown ordered all flags in California to be flown at half-staff, and called Milk a "very hard-working and dedicated supervisor, a leader of San Francisco's gay community, who kept his promise to represent all of his constituents". President Jimmy Carter expressed his shock at both murders and sent his condolences. California Assembly Speaker Leo McCarthy called it "an insane tragedy". "A City in Agony" was the main headline in *The San Francisco Examiner* the day after the murders; inside the paper, stories of the killings under the headline "Black Monday" were printed one after the other with updates of the bodies being shipped home from Guyana. An editorial describing "A city with more sorrow and despair in its heart than any city should have to endure" went on to ask how such tragedies occur, particularly for "men of such sympathy and vision and great energies." Dan White was charged with two counts of murder and held without bail, subject to the death penalty, due to the recent passage of a state proposition allowing the death penalty or life imprisonment for the murder of a public official. An analysis of the months surrounding the murders called 1978 and 1979 "the most emotionally devastating years in San Francisco's admittedly fabulous history."

White, 32, who had been in the army during the Vietnam War, had pursued a tough platform against crime in his district. Colleagues declared him a typical middle-class American ("all-American boy"). He was to receive an award the following week for having rescued a woman and a child from a burning building when he was a firefighter in 1977. Although he was the only one to vote against Milk's gay rights bill earlier that year, he had been quoted as saying, "I respect the rights of all people, including gays". Milk and White initially hit it off. One of White's political advisors (who was gay) recalled, "Dan had more in common with Harvey than with anyone else on the council." White voted in favor of a support center for elderly gays, as well as to honor the 25th anniversary of the pioneering work of Del Martin and Phyllis Lyon.

After Milk's vote for the mental health center in White's district, however, White refused to speak to Milk and only communicated with someone from Milk's office. Other acquaintances remembered White as being very intense. "He was impulsive ... He was an extremely competitive man, obsessively so... I don't think he could accept defeat," San Francisco's fire aid chief told reporters. White's first campaign manager left in the middle of the campaign, and told a reporter that White was an egotist and it was clear that he was antigay, but he denied it in the press. White's allies and supporters described him "as a man with a pugilistic temper and an uncanny ability to nurse a grudge". The aide who liaised between White and Milk recalled: "Talking to him, I realized that he saw Harvey Milk and George Moscone as representing everything that was wrong with the world".

When Milk's friends searched his closet for a suit for his coffin, they learned how much he had been affected by the recent decline in his performance as a supervisor. All his clothes were left out, all his socks had holes in them. He was cremated and his ashes were divided up, most of them scattered in San Francisco Bay by his closest friends. Some of them were condensed and buried under the sidewalk in front of 575 Castro Street, where Castro Camera had been located. Harry Britt, one of the four people Milk listed on his cassette tape as an acceptable replacement if he were assassinated, was chosen by the acting mayor, Dianne Feinstein.

Judgment

The arrest and trial of Dan White caused a sensation, and illustrated serious tensions between the liberal population and the city police. The San Francisco police were mostly made up of working-class Irish descendants who were intensely disgusted by the growing gay immigration, as well as the liberal orientation of the city government. After White turned himself in and confessed, he sat in his cell while his former police colleagues made jokes about Harvey Milk; the police openly wore "Free Dan White" T-shirts in the days following the murder. A San Francisco deputy sheriff later stated: "The more I observed what was going on in the jail, the more I began to stop seeing what Dan White did as the act of an individual and began to see it as a political act in a political movement." White showed no remorse for his actions, and only displayed vulnerability during the eight-minute phone call from prison to his mother.

The jury for White's trial was made up of white middle-class San Franciscans, who were mostly Catholic; homosexuals and ethnic minorities were excluded in the jury selection. The jury was clearly sympathetic to the defendant: some of the members cried when they heard the recording of White's moving confession, at the end of which the interrogator thanked White for his honesty. White's defense lawyer, Doug Schmidt, claimed that he was not responsible for his actions, using the legal defense known as diminished capacity: "Good people, fine people, with great records, just don't kill people in cold blood." Schmidt tried to prove that White's distressed mental state was a result of manipulation by the politicians on the City Council, who had consistently let him down and confused him, finally promising to give him his job back only to refuse him again. Schmidt said that White's mental deterioration was demonstrated and aggravated by unhealthy food consumption the night before the murders, as he was generally known to be conscious of his dietary health. Regional newspapers quickly dubbed her the "twinkie defense" (a kind of cake with filling, common in the United States). White was acquitted of the murders (felony murder charges) on May 21, 1979, but found guilty of manslaughter of the two victims, and was sentenced to seven and two-thirds years in prison. With his sentence reduced for good behavior and time spent working in prison, he would be released in five. He cried when he heard the verdict.

The White night riots

Acting Mayor Feinstein, Supervisor Carol Ruth Silver, and Milk's successor, Harry Britt, condemned the jury's decision. When it was announced on the police radio in the city, someone sang "Danny Boy" in the police band. An avalanche of people from the Castro District walked back to City Hall chanting "Avenge Harvey Milk" and "He got away with murder". The pandemonium quickly escalated when rocks were thrown in front of the building's doors. Milk's friends and advisors tried to stop the destruction, but the crowd of over three thousand ignored them and set fire to police cars. They pushed a burning newspaper garbage can through the broken doors of City Hall and then cheered as the flames grew. One of the protesters answered a reporter's question about why they were destroying parts of the city: "Just tell people that we eat too many twinkies. That's why this is happening." The police chief ordered the officers not to retaliate, but to stand their ground. The White night riots, as they became known, lasted several hours.

Later that night, May 21, 1979, several police cars filled with officers wearing riot gear arrived at the Elephant Walk Bar on Castro Street. Harvey Milk disciple Cleve Jones, and a reporter for the *San Francisco Chronicle*, Warren Hinckle, watched as officers stormed the bar and began beating customers at random. After 15 minutes of fighting, they left the bar and attacked people walking along the street. The police chief finally ordered the officers to leave the neighborhood. By morning, 61 police officers and 100 protesters and gay Castro residents had been hospitalized. City Hall, police vehicles and the Elephant Walk Bar suffered more than a million dollars in damage.

After the verdict, district attorney José Freitas faced a furious gay community to explain what had gone wrong. The prosecutor admitted to feeling sorry for White before the trial, and to failing to ask the interrogator who recorded White's confession (and who was a childhood friend of White's and coach of his police softball team) about his prejudices and the support White received from the police, because, he said, he didn't want to embarrass the detective in front of his family in court. Freitas also didn't ask questions about White's state of mind, lack of a history of mental illness, or bring up city politics, suggesting that revenge might have been a motive. Supervisor Carol Ruth Silver testified on the last day of the trial that White and Milk were not friendly, but she had contacted the DA's office and insisted on testifying. It was the only testimony the jury heard about their strained relationship. Freitas blamed the jurors, saying they had been "taken over by the whole emotional aspect of the trial".

Consequences

The Milk and Moscone murders and the White trial changed city politics and the legal system in California. In 1980 San Francisco ended supervisor elections by district, fearing that such a divided Board of Supervisors would be detrimental to the city, and that this had been a factor in the murders. A grassroots neighborhood effort to restore district elections in the mid-1990s was successful, and the city returned to neighborhood representatives in 2000. As a result of the Dan White trial, California voters changed the law to reduce the likelihood of acquittal for defendants who knew what they were doing but claimed their capacity was impaired. Impaired capacity was abolished as a defense to a charge, but courts accepted this evidence when deciding whether a convicted defendant should be incarcerated, committed to a mental hospital, or receive other punishment. The "twinkie defense" entered American mythology, popularly described as a case in which a murderer escapes justice because he committed unhealthy dietary excesses, simplifying White's lack of political skill, his relationship with George Moscone and Harvey Milk, and what *San Francisco Chronicle* columnist Herb Caen described as a pandemic "homosexual aversion" on the part of the police.

Dan White served his sentence for the double murder of Moscone and Milk for just over five years. On October 22, 1985, a year and a half after his release from prison, White was found dead in a running car in his ex-wife's garage. He was 39 years old. His defense lawyer told reporters that he had been devastated by the loss of his family, and the situation he had caused, adding "This was a sick man".

Legacy

Politics

Harvey Milk's political career focused on making governments responsive to individuals, gay liberation and the importance of neighborhoods to the city. At the beginning of each campaign, an issue was added to Milk's public policy philosophy. His 1973 campaign focused on the first point, that as a small businessman in San Francisco - a city dominated by large corporations, which had been courted by the city government - his interests were being ignored because he was not represented by a large financial institution. Although he didn't hide the fact that he was gay, it didn't become an issue until his campaign for the California State Assembly in 1976. It was brought to the fore in the campaign for supervisor against Rick Stokes, because it was an extension of his ideas of individual freedom.

Milk strongly believed that neighborhoods promoted unity and a small-town experience, and that the Castro should provide services to all its residents. He opposed the closing of an elementary school; although most gay people in the Castro did not have children, Milk saw that his neighborhood had the potential to welcome everyone. He told his aides to focus on fixing potholes in the streets, and boasted that 50 new stop signs had been installed in District 5. Responding to city residents' biggest complaint about life in San Francisco - dog feces - Milk made it a priority to enact a law requiring dog owners to take care of their animals' excrement. Randy Shilts noted that "some claim Harvey was a socialist or various other kinds of ideologues, but in reality Harvey's political philosophy was never more complicated than the issue of dog excrement; government should solve the basic problems of the people."

Karen Foss, a communications professor at the University of New Mexico, attributes Milk's impact on San Francisco politics to the fact that he was unlike anyone else who held public office in the city. She writes, "Milk came to be a charismatic and highly energetic figure with a taste for theater and nothing to lose ... Using laughter, reversal, transcendence, and his included/excluded status, Milk helped create a climate in which dialogue about issues became possible. He also provided a means to integrate the disparate voices of his varied constituents." Milk had been a fiery speaker from the time he began campaigning in 1973, and his oratorical skills only improved after he became town supervisor. His most famous talking points became known as the "Hope Speech," which became a staple throughout his political career. It opened with a joke about the accusation that homosexuals were recruiting impressionable young men to their side: "My name is Harvey Milk - and I want to recruit you." A version of the Speech of Hope that he made towards the end of his life was considered by his friends and advisors to be the best, and in closing the most effective:

In the last year of his life, Milk stressed that homosexual people should be more visible to help end discrimination and violence against them. Although Milk had not come out to his mother before his death many years earlier, in his final statement during his recording predicting his assassination, he urged others to do so:

However, Milk's assassination has become intertwined with his political effectiveness, partly because he was killed at the height of his popularity. Historian Neil Miller writes: "No contemporary gay American leader has yet to achieve in life the stature that Milk found in death". His legacy has become ambiguous; Randy Shilts concludes his biography by writing that Milk's success, murder, and the inevitable injustice of the White verdict represent the experience of all gays. Milk's life was "a metaphor for the homosexual experience in America". According to Francisca FitzGerald, Milk's legend has been unable to be sustained just as no one has seemed able to take his place in the years since his death: "Castro saw him as a martyr, but understood his martyrdom as an end rather than a beginning. He had died, and with him a large part of Castro's optimism, idealism and ambition seemed to die too. Castro couldn't find anyone to take his place in his affection and, possibly, he didn't want anyone." On the twentieth anniversary of Milk's death, historian John D'Emilio said, "The legacy I think he would want to be remembered for is the imperative to live a life at all times with integrity." For such a short political career, Cleve Jones attributes more to his assassination than his life: "His assassination and the response to it made permanent and indisputable the full participation of gays and lesbians in the political process." In 2009, the governor of California, Arnold Schwarzenegger, decreed that May 22, the date of Milk's birth, is Harvey Milk Day. It is a day to honor the first openly gay politician elected in the United States.

Tributes and representations in culture

The city of San Francisco paid tribute to Milk by naming several places after him. Where Market and Castro Streets intersect in San Francisco, a huge gay pride flag flies in Harvey Milk Square. The San Francisco Gay Democratic Club changed its name to the Harvey Milk Memorial Gay Democratic Club in 1978 and prides itself on being the largest democratic organization in San Francisco. In New York, Harvey Milk High School is a school program for at-risk youth that focuses on the needs of gay, lesbian, bisexual and transgender students and operates out of the Hetrick Martin Institute.

In 1982, freelance reporter Randy Shilts completed his first book: a biography of Milk, entitled *The Mayor of Castro Street*. Shilts wrote the book while unable to find steady employment as an openly gay reporter. *The Times of Harvey Milk*, a documentary based on material from the book, won the 1984 Oscar for best documentary. Director Rob Epstein later spoke about why he chose Milk's life as the subject: "At the time, for those of us who lived in San Francisco, it felt like this was life-changing, that all eyes in the world were on us, but in fact most of the world outside San Francisco had no idea. It was just a really brief, provincial, localized current events story in which the mayor and a member of the San Francisco city council were killed. It didn't have a lot of repercussions." The musical theater production entitled *The Harvey Milk Show* premiered in 1991. *Harvey Milk*, an opera written by Stewart Wallace, which "mystifies Milk as a symbol for the birth of the modern gay rights movement", premiered in 1996. A biographical film about Milk's life was released in 2008 after 15 years in production; it was directed by Gus Van Sant and starred Sean Penn as Milk and Josh Brolin as Dan White, winning two Oscars, for Best Original Screenplay and Best Actor. The film was shot in eight weeks, and often used extras that were images of real events in crowd scenes, including a scene depicting Milk's "Speech of Hope" at the 1978 Gay Parade.

Milk was included in *Time Magazine*'s "100 Heroes and Icons of the 20th Century" as "a symbol of what gays can accomplish and the dangers they face in doing so". Despite his grotesque and public stunts, "no one understood how his public role could affect private lives better than Milk ... [he] knew that the root cause of the problem was gay invisibility." *The Advocate* magazine listed Milk third in its edition on the "40 heroes" of the 20th century, quoting Dianne Feinstein: "His homosexuality gave him insight into the scars that all oppressed people bear. He believed that no sacrifice was too great a price to pay for the cause of human rights." Harry Britt summed up Milk's impact on the night he was shot in 1978: "No matter what the world has taught us about ourselves, we can be beautiful and we can achieve our things together ... Harvey was a prophet ... he lived by a vision ... Something very special is going to happen in this city and it will have Harvey Milk's name on it."

Other books by United Library

https://campsite.bio/unitedlibrary

Milton Keynes UK
Ingram Content Group UK Ltd.
UKHW020627080324
438959UK00015B/672